Spiralizer Cookbook

Ketogenic Friendly, Low-Carb, High-Protein Meat & Fish Spiralizer Recipes for a Whole Family

(Spiralize Everything Book 5)

Legal & Disclaimer

The information contained in this book and its contents is not designed to replace or take the place of any form of medical or professional advice; and is not meant to replace the need for independent medical, financial, legal or other professional advice or services, as may be required. The content and information in this book has been provided for educational and entertainment purposes only.

The content and information contained in this book has been compiled from sources deemed reliable, and it is accurate to the best of the Author's knowledge, information, and belief. However, the Author cannot guarantee its accuracy and validity and cannot be held liable for any errors and/or omissions. Further, changes are periodically made to this book as and when needed. Where appropriate and/or necessary, you must consult a professional (including but not limited to your doctor, attorney, financial advisor or such other professional advisor) before using any of the suggested remedies, techniques, or information in this book.

Upon using the contents and information contained in this book, you agree to hold harmless the Author from and against any damages, costs, and expenses, including any legal fees potentially resulting from the application of any of the information provided by this book. This disclaimer applies to any loss, damages or injury caused by the use and application, whether directly or indirectly, of any advice or information presented, whether for breach of contract, tort, negligence, personal injury, criminal intent, or under any other cause of action.

You agree to accept all risks of using the information presented in this book.

Table of Contents

Introduction

This cookbook contains different meat and fish spiralizer recipes with various spiralized or grated vegetables and fruits. You will find interesting recipes that will inspire you to cook fantastic spiralized dishes. You should use your imagination because there is no limit to what you can prepare when using meat, fish and spiralized vegetables as the main ingredient. This spiralizer recipe book was created to inspire you to discover a colorful world of fish and meat spiralizer cooking!

Moreover, you don't need to be a professional 28 Michelin Star chef to use fish, meat and spiralized vegetables from this cooking book and to cook spiralized dishes for yourself or your family. I would like to encourage you to test new spiralizer recipes and experiment by adding your own flavors!

Kitchen Utensils That You Will Need to Cook Spiralizer Recipes

To prepare delicious spiralizer dishes you will need to have the right tools in your kitchen. The following list of kitchen tools will be helpful.

Spiralizer

Spiralizer is the main kitchen tool that you will need to prepare tasty spiralized recipes. Remember that sometimes you can use Korean style grater as well.

Food Scale

The food scale is the main tool. You will use it to measure any food, especially fish – salmon, mahi-mahi, tuna or cod. As well as turkey, pork, goat, beef, lamb ribs or vegetables. It will always show you the quantity of ingredients that you need for spiralizer dishes.

Food Processor or Blender

Having a food processor or blender is crucial. It will help you to process, pulse, and blend nuts, vegetables or fruits.

Electric Hand Mixer

Electric hand mixer will save your energy and of course time, especially when you are preparing spiralizer recipes where you need to combine various ingredients.

Pot, Saucepan, Frying Pan or Wok

Having a large pot, saucepan, frying pan, skillet or wok in your kitchen is crucial when preparing tasty spiralizer dishes because you will fry, bake, melt, mix and boil all the ingredients there.

Knife Sharpening Stone or Sharp Knife

When preparing spiralizer recipes you often need to cut, chop, slice or halve meat, fish, fresh vegetables or fruits. In this case, having a sharp blade in your kitchen will save you a lot of time because you will finish cutting up your ingredients much faster than you would if using a dull knife.

Baking pan

Baking pan is also important because you will need it to bake the meat, fish and spiralized vegetables.

The following chapters contain tasty spiralizer recipes that will have your taste buds come to life!

Spiralized Meat & Fish Dishes

Spiralized Beets with Cod, Zucchini and Apricots

Prep Time: 25 min. | Cooking Time: 40-50 min. | Servings: 3

Ingredients:

15 oz cod, cubed

4 beets, peeled and spiralized

1 zucchini, peeled and spiralized

4 garlic cloves, minced

5 tablespoons Olive oil

1 cup of apricots

salt and pepper

1 teaspoon powdered black pepper

2 tablespoons powdered garlic

1 teaspoon nutmeg, ground

1 bunch of fresh parsley, chopped

How to Prepare:

1. Wash and soak the apricots in the warm water and then chop them.

2. Combine the powdered black pepper, powdered garlic and some salt. Season the codfish with the salt and pepper, and toss in the powdered garlic, and nutmeg mix. Marinate the fish cubes overnight in the powdered garlic, pepper, and nutmeg.

3. Heat the oil and fry the cod for 15 minutes. In a frying pan or wok, combine the codfish with the spiralized beets and fry the fish with the beets for around 30 minutes, until golden brown.

4. Toss the spiralized zucchini in the Olive oil. 10 minutes before the code cubes and beets are ready, mix in the spiralized zucchini and stew with the fish and beets with the lid closed for around 10 minutes, until the liquid is absorbed. A few minutes before the code cubes are ready, add in the minced garlic cloves and chopped apricots.

5. Sprinkle the chopped parsley and you are free to serve the fish and spiralized beets in separate plates with the white or red wine. Remember that this dish should be served warm.

Nutritional Information:

Calories: 165; Total fat: 30 oz; Total carbohydrates: 37 oz; Protein: 20 oz

Spiralized Zucchini with Tuna, Pineapple and Raisins

Prep Time: 25 min. | Cooking Time: 40-50 min. | Servings: 4

Ingredients:

30 oz tuna, cubed

2 big zucchinis, peeled and spiralized

8 pineapple rings

4 garlic cloves, minced

5 tablespoons Olive oil

2 cups of raisins

salt and pepper

1 teaspoon powdered black pepper

2 tablespoons powdered garlic

1 teaspoon nutmeg, ground

1 bunch of fresh parsley, chopped

How to Prepare:

1. Wash and soak the raisins in the warm water.

2. Combine the powdered black pepper, powdered garlic and some salt. Season the tuna cubes with the salt and pepper, and toss in the powdered garlic, and nutmeg mix. Marinate the fish cubes overnight in the powdered garlic, pepper, and nutmeg.

3. Heat the oil and fry the tuna for 15 minutes. In a frying pan or wok, combine the tuna cubes with the spiralized zucchini and fry the fish with the zucchini for around 30 minutes, until golden brown.

4. 10 minutes before the tuna cubes and zucchini is ready, mix in the pineapple rings and stew with the fish and zucchini with the lid closed for around 10 minutes, until the liquid is absorbed. A few minutes before the tuna cubes are ready, mix in the minced garlic cloves and raisins.

5. Sprinkle the chopped parsley and you are free to serve the fish and spiralized zucchini in separate plates with the white wine or cold beer. Remember that this dish should be served warm.

Nutritional Information:

Calories: 188; Total fat: 32 oz; Total carbohydrates: 38 oz; Protein: 27 oz

Spiralized Potatoes with Salmon, Pineapple and Lemon

Prep Time: 25 min. | Cooking Time: 40-50 min. | Servings: 2

Ingredients:

20 oz salmon cubes

8 medium potatoes, peeled and spiralized

2 cups of pineapple, cubed

4 garlic cloves, minced

5 tablespoons Olive oil

2 cups of raisins

salt and pepper

1 teaspoon powdered black pepper

2 tablespoons powdered garlic

3 tablespoons freshly squeezed lemon juice

1 bunch of fresh parsley, chopped

How to Prepare:

1. Wash and soak the raisins in the warm water.

2. Combine the powdered black pepper, powdered garlic and some salt. Season the salmon cubes with the salt and pepper, and toss in the powdered garlic, and pepper mix. Then sprinkle the lemon juice on top. Marinate the fish cubes overnight in the powdered garlic, pepper, and lemon juice.

3. Heat the oil and fry the salmon for 10 minutes. In a frying pan or wok, combine the salmon cubes with the spiralized potatoes. Fry and stew the fish with the potatoes for around 30 minutes, until the salmon is golden brown.

4. 10 minutes before the salmon cubes and potatoes are ready, mix in the pineapple cubes and stew with the fish and potatoes with the lid closed for around 10 minutes, until the liquid is absorbed. A few minutes before the salmon cubes are ready, mix in the minced garlic cloves and raisins.

5. Sprinkle the chopped parsley and you are free to serve the fish and spiralized potatoes in separate

plates with the white wine or cold beer. Remember that this dish should be served warm.

<u>Nutritional Information:</u>

Calories: 180; Total fat: 30 oz; Total carbohydrates: 35 oz; Protein: 23 oz

Spiralized Sweet Potatoes with Rainbow Trout, Squash and Lemon

Prep Time: 25 min. | Cooking Time: 40-50 min. | Servings: 2

Ingredients:

2 rainbow trouts

10 sweet potatoes, peeled and spiralized

1 squash, peeled and spiralized

4 garlic cloves, minced

5 tablespoons Olive oil

salt and pepper

1 teaspoon powdered black pepper

1 teaspoon powdered red pepper

2 tablespoons powdered garlic

3 tablespoons freshly squeezed lemon juice

1 bunch of fresh chives, chopped

How to Prepare:

1. Combine the powdered black pepper, red pepper, powdered garlic and some salt. Season the rainbow trout with the salt and pepper, and toss in the powdered garlic, and pepper mix. Then sprinkle the lemon juice on top. Marinate the fish overnight in the powdered garlic, pepper, and lemon juice.

2. Heat the oil and fry the rainbow trout for 30 minutes. 10 minutes before the trout is ready, mix in the spiralized squash and stew with the fish with the lid closed for around 10 minutes, until the liquid is absorbed. A few minutes before the fish is ready, mix in the minced garlic cloves.

3. Meanwhile, in a second skillet or wok, fry the spiralized sweet potatoes. Fry the sweet potatoes for around 20 minutes, until golden brown.

4. Sprinkle the chopped chives and you are free to serve the fish with the spiralized sweet potatoes, squash and fresh greenery. Remember that this dish could be served warm.

Nutritional Information:

Calories: 184; Total fat: 34 oz; Total carbohydrates: 40 oz; Protein: 28 oz

Spiralized Zucchini with Rainbow Trout, Squash and Oranges

Prep Time: 25 min. | Cooking Time: 40-50 min. | Servings: 4

Ingredients:

4 rainbow trouts

2 zucchinis, peeled and spiralized

1 squash, peeled and spiralized

3 cups of oranges, cubed

4 garlic cloves, minced

5 tablespoons Olive oil

salt and pepper

1 teaspoon powdered black pepper

1 teaspoon powdered red pepper

2 tablespoons powdered garlic

5 tablespoons freshly squeezed orange juice

1 bunch of fresh chives, chopped

How to Prepare:

1. Combine the powdered black pepper, red pepper, powdered garlic and some salt. Season the rainbow trout with the salt and pepper, and toss in the powdered garlic, and pepper mix. Then sprinkle the orange juice on top. Marinate the fish overnight in the powdered garlic, pepper, and orange juice.

2. Heat the oil and fry the rainbow trout for 30 minutes. 10 minutes before the trout is ready, mix in the spiralized squash and stew with the fish with the lid closed for around 10 minutes, until the liquid is absorbed. A few minutes before the fish is ready, mix in the minced garlic cloves.

3. Meanwhile, in a second skillet or wok, stew the spiralized zucchini. Stew the zucchini for around 20 minutes.

4. Add in the cubed oranges. Sprinkle the chopped chives and you are free to serve the fish with the spiralized zucchini and the fresh greenery. Remember that this dish could be served warm.

Nutritional Information:

Calories: 185; Total fat: 36 oz; Total carbohydrates: 44 oz;

Protein: 31 oz

Spiralized Zucchini with Mackerel, Squash and Peanuts

Prep Time: 25 min. | Cooking Time: 40-50 min. | Servings: 2

Ingredients:

2 mackerels

2 zucchinis, peeled and spiralized

1 squash, peeled and spiralized

2 cups of peanuts

5 garlic cloves, minced

5 tablespoons Olive oil

salt and pepper

1 teaspoon powdered black pepper

1 teaspoon powdered red pepper

2 tablespoons powdered garlic

5 tablespoons freshly squeezed lemon juice

1 bunch of fresh chives, chopped

How to Prepare:

1. Preheat the oven to 220°-250° Fahrenheit and roast the peanuts in the oven for around 10 minutes until lightly browned and crispy.

2. Combine the powdered black pepper, red pepper, powdered garlic and some salt. Season the mackerel with the salt and pepper, and toss in the powdered garlic, and pepper mix. Then pour the lemon juice on top. Marinate the fish overnight in the powdered garlic, pepper, and lemon juice.

3. Heat the oil and fry the mackerel for 30 minutes. 10 minutes before the mackerel is ready, mix in the spiralized squash and stew with the fish with the lid closed for around 10 minutes, until the liquid is absorbed. A few minutes before the fish is ready, mix in the minced garlic cloves.

4. Meanwhile, in a second skillet or wok, stew the spiralized zucchini. Stew the zucchini for around 20 minutes.

5. Mix in the peanuts. Sprinkle the chopped chives and you are free to serve the mackerel with the spiralized zucchini and the fresh greenery. Remember that this dish could be served warm.

Nutritional Information:

Calories: 190; Total fat: 38 oz; Total carbohydrates: 48 oz; Protein: 37 oz

Inspiralized Zucchini with Lamb, Onion, Porter and Parsley

Prep Time: 20 min. | Cooking Time: 60-70 min. | Servings: 3

Ingredients:

20 oz lamb, cubed

3 bottles of dark beer, Porter or Belgian Style Beer with coriander (Chinese parsley)

5 onions, peeled and chopped

2 bunches of parsley, chopped

2 cups of peanuts

2 big zucchinis, peeled and spiralized

7 tablespoons Olive oil

7 tablespoons freshly squeezed lemon juice

1 teaspoon powdered red pepper

2 tablespoons powdered garlic

1 teaspoon nutmeg & basil, ground

salt and pepper

How to Prepare:

1. Preheat the oven to 230°-240° Fahrenheit and roast the peanuts in the oven for around 10-15 minutes until lightly browned and crispy, then grind the peanuts using a food processor.

2. In a bowl, combine powdered red pepper, powdered garlic, nutmeg, basil, and some salt. Season the lamb cubes with the salt and pepper, and toss in the powdered garlic, powdered red pepper, basil, onions, parsley and nutmeg mix. Set the meat aside

to marinate it overnight in Porter or Belgian Style Beer with the coriander and spices.

3. Preheat the oven to 330°-350° Fahrenheit, and bake the cubed lamb meat for around 50-70 minutes until golden brown and crispy. Toss the spiralized zucchini in the Olive oil and salt. 10-15 minutes before the lamb meat is ready mix in the spiralized zucchini and bake it with the lamb chunks.

4. Spoon the peanuts over the spiralized zucchini and baked lamb chunks, sprinkle the salt and pepper and pour the freshly squeezed lemon juice over the lamb. You are free to serve the spiralized zucchini with the lamb in separate plates with a cold beer. Remember that this dish should be served warm.

Nutritional Information:

Calories: 365; Total fat: 44 oz; Total carbohydrates: 76 oz; Protein: 40 oz

Spiralized Zucchini with Pork, Onion, Dark Beer and Parsley

Prep Time: 20 min. | Cooking Time: 50-60 min. | Servings: 3

Ingredients:

25 oz pork, cubed

3 bottles of dark beer, Porter or Belgian Style Beer with coriander (Chinese parsley)

5 onions, peeled and chopped

2 bunches of parsley, chopped

2 cups of peanuts

2 big zucchinis, peeled and spiralized

7 tablespoons Olive oil

7 tablespoons freshly squeezed lemon juice

1 teaspoon powdered red pepper

2 tablespoons powdered garlic

1 teaspoon nutmeg & basil, ground

salt and pepper

How to Prepare:

1. Preheat the oven to 230°-240° Fahrenheit and roast the peanuts in the oven for around 10-15 minutes until lightly browned and crispy, then grind the peanuts using a food processor.

2. In a bowl, combine powdered red pepper, powdered garlic, nutmeg, basil, and some salt. Season the pork cubes with the salt and pepper, and toss in the powdered garlic, powdered red pepper, basil, onions, parsley and nutmeg mix. Set the meat aside to marinate it overnight in Porter or Belgian Style Beer with the coriander and spices.

3. Preheat the oven to 320°-340° Fahrenheit, and bake the cubed pork meat for around 50-60 minutes until golden brown and crispy. Toss the spiralized zucchini in the Olive oil and salt. 10-15 minutes before the pork meat is ready mix in the spiralized zucchini and bake it with the pork chunks.

4. Spoon the peanuts over the spiralized zucchini and baked pork chunks, sprinkle the salt and pepper and

pour the freshly squeezed lemon juice over the pork. You are free to serve the spiralized zucchini with the pork in separate plates with a cold beer and potatoes. Remember that this dish should be served warm.

Nutritional Information:

Calories: 365; Total fat: 44 oz; Total carbohydrates: 76 oz; Protein: 40 oz

Spiralized Pumpkin with Lamb, Onion, Wine and Parsley

Prep Time: 20 min. | Cooking Time: 60-70 min. | Servings: 3

Ingredients:

20 oz lamb, cubed

2 cups of pumpkin, peeled and spiralized

1 bottle of white wine

5 onions, peeled and chopped

2 bunches of parsley, chopped

2 cups of peanuts

7 tablespoons Olive oil

7 tablespoons freshly squeezed lemon juice

1 teaspoon powdered red pepper

2 tablespoons powdered garlic

1 teaspoon nutmeg & basil, ground

salt and pepper

How to Prepare:

1. Preheat the oven to 230°-240° Fahrenheit and roast the peanuts in the oven for around 10-15 minutes until lightly browned and crispy, then grind the peanuts using a food processor.

2. In a bowl, combine powdered red pepper, powdered garlic, nutmeg, basil, and some salt. Season the lamb cubes with the salt and pepper, and toss in the powdered garlic, powdered red pepper, basil, onions, parsley and nutmeg mix. Set the meat aside to marinate it overnight in white wine and spices.

3. Preheat the oven to 330°-350° Fahrenheit, and bake the cubed lamb meat for around 50-60 minutes until golden brown and crispy. Toss the spiralized pumpkin in the Olive oil and salt. 10-15 minutes before the lamb meat is ready mix in the spiralized pumpkin and bake it with the lamb chunks.

4. Spoon the peanuts over the spiralized pumpkin and baked lamb chunks, sprinkle the salt and pepper

and pour the freshly squeezed lemon juice over the lamb. You are free to serve the spiralized pumpkin with the lamb in separate plates with a white wine. Remember that this dish should be served warm.

Nutritional Information:

Calories: 364; Total fat: 43 oz; Total carbohydrates: 74 oz; Protein: 39 oz

Spiralized Pumpkin with Beef, Onion, Wine and Parsley

Prep Time: 20 min. | Cooking Time: 60-70 min. | Servings: 4

Ingredients:

20 oz beef, cubed

3 cups of pumpkin, peeled and spiralized

1 bottle of white wine

5 onions, peeled and chopped

2 bunches of parsley, chopped

2 cups of walnuts

7 tablespoons Olive oil

7 tablespoons freshly squeezed lemon juice

1 teaspoon powdered red pepper

2 tablespoons powdered garlic

1 teaspoon nutmeg & basil, ground

salt and pepper

How to Prepare:

1. Preheat the oven to 250°-270° Fahrenheit and roast the walnuts in the oven for around 10-15 minutes until lightly browned and crispy, then grind the walnuts using a food processor.

2. In a bowl, combine powdered red pepper, powdered garlic, nutmeg, basil, and some salt. Season the lamb cubes with the salt and pepper, and toss in the powdered garlic, powdered red pepper, basil, onions, parsley and nutmeg mix. Set the meat aside to marinate it overnight in white wine and spices.

3. Preheat the oven to 330°-350° Fahrenheit, and bake the cubed lamb meat for around 50-60 minutes until golden brown and crispy. Toss the spiralized pumpkin in the Olive oil and salt. 10-15 minutes before the lamb meat is ready mix in the spiralized pumpkin and bake it with the lamb chunks.

4. Spoon the walnuts over the spiralized pumpkin and baked lamb chunks, sprinkle the salt and pepper and pour the freshly squeezed lemon juice over the lamb. You are free to serve the spiralized pumpkin with the lamb in separate plates with a white wine. Remember that this dish should be served warm.

Nutritional Information:

Calories: 367; Total fat: 44 oz; Total carbohydrates: 75 oz; Protein: 40 oz

Spiralized Squash with Beef, Beans, Walnuts and Garlic

Prep Time: 20 min. | Cooking Time: 60-70 min. | Servings: 4

Ingredients:

20 oz beef, cubed

3 cups of squash, peeled and spiralized

2 cups of red beans

15 garlic cloves, peeled and chopped

2 cups of walnuts

5 tablespoons Olive oil

7 tablespoons freshly squeezed lemon juice

1 teaspoon powdered red pepper

2 tablespoons powdered garlic

1 teaspoon nutmeg & basil, ground

salt and pepper

How to Prepare:

1. Soak the red beans in the warm water overnight and then boil them.

2. Preheat the oven to 250°-270° Fahrenheit and roast the walnuts in the oven for around 10-15 minutes until lightly browned and crispy, then grind the walnuts using a food processor.

3. In a bowl, combine powdered red pepper, powdered garlic, nutmeg, basil, and some salt. Season the beef cubes with the salt and pepper, and toss in the powdered garlic, powdered red pepper, basil, garlic, and nutmeg mix. Set the beef meat aside to marinate it overnight in garlic and spices.

4. Preheat the oven to 330°-350° Fahrenheit, and bake the cubed beef meat for around 50-60 minutes until golden brown and crispy. Toss the spiralized squash in the Olive oil and salt. 10-15 minutes before the beef meat is ready mix in the spiralized squash and boiled red beans. Bake the vegetables with the beef chunks.

5. Spoon the walnuts over the spiralized squash and baked beef chunks, sprinkle the salt and pepper and pour the freshly squeezed lemon juice over the beef. You are free to serve the spiralized squash with the beef in separate plates with a white wine. Remember that this dish should be served warm.

Nutritional Information:

Calories: 366; Total fat: 43 oz; Total carbohydrates: 73 oz; Protein: 38 oz

Spiralized Cabbage with Beef, Beans, Walnuts and Garlic

Prep Time: 20 min. | Cooking Time: 60-70 min. | Servings: 4

Ingredients:

20 oz beef, cubed

4 cups of cabbage, peeled and spiralized

2 cups of red beans

15 garlic cloves, peeled and chopped

2 cups of walnuts

5 tablespoons Olive oil

7 tablespoons freshly squeezed lemon juice

1 teaspoon powdered red pepper

2 tablespoons powdered garlic

1 teaspoon nutmeg & basil, ground

salt and pepper

How to Prepare:

1. Soak the red beans in the warm water overnight and then boil them.

2. Preheat the oven to 250°-270° Fahrenheit and roast the walnuts in the oven for around 10-15 minutes until lightly browned and crispy, then grind the walnuts using a food processor.

3. In a bowl, combine powdered red pepper, powdered garlic, nutmeg, basil, and some salt. Season the beef cubes with the salt and pepper, and toss in the powdered garlic, powdered red pepper, basil, garlic, and nutmeg mix. Set the beef meat aside to marinate it overnight in garlic and spices.

4. Preheat the oven to 330°-350° Fahrenheit, and bake the cubed beef meat for around 50-60 minutes until golden brown and crispy. Toss the spiralized cabbage in the Olive oil and salt. 10-15 minutes before the beef meat is ready mix in the spiralized cabbage and boiled red beans. Bake the vegetables with the beef chunks.

5. Spoon the walnuts over the spiralized cabbage and baked beef chunks, sprinkle the salt and pepper and pour the freshly squeezed lemon juice over the beef. You are free to serve the spiralized cabbage with the beef in separate plates with a white wine. Remember that this dish should be served warm.

Nutritional Information:

Calories: 367; Total fat: 44 oz; Total carbohydrates: 75 oz; Protein: 39 oz

Spiralized Potatoes with Goat Ribs and Carrots

Prep Time: 25 min. | Cooking Time: 60-70 min. | Servings: 4

Ingredients:

20 oz goat ribs

10 potatoes, peeled and spiralized

5 carrots, peeled and spiralized

5 tomatoes, cubed

6 tablespoons Olive oil

5 tablespoons freshly squeezed lemon juice

2 teaspoons powdered red pepper

4 tablespoons powdered garlic

1 teaspoon nutmeg, ground

salt and pepper

How to Prepare:

1. In a bowl, combine powdered red pepper, powdered garlic, nutmeg, some salt and pepper. Mix well. Then season the goat ribs with the salt and pepper, and toss in the powdered garlic, powdered red pepper, and nutmeg mix. Set the goat meat aside and marinate it 24 hours in spices.

2. Heat the Olive oil in a frying pan or wok and stew the goat ribs for around 20 minutes. Preheat the oven to 325°-345° Fahrenheit, and bake the ribs for around 60-70 minutes until golden brown and crispy. Toss the spiralized potatoes and carrots in the Olive oil and salt. 20-25 minutes before the goat ribs are ready add in the spiralized potatoes and

carrots and bake them with the goat ribs and vegetables.

3. Mix in the cubed tomatoes and sprinkle the salt and pepper. Pour the freshly squeezed lemon juice over the goat ribs and you are free to serve the spiralized potatoes and carrots with goat in separate plates with the tomato sauce and white wine. Remember that this dish should be served warm.

Nutritional Information:

Calories: 345; Total fat: 55 oz; Total carbohydrates: 84 oz; Protein: 45 oz

Spiralized Sweet Potatoes with Goat Ribs, Squash and Lemon

Prep Time: 25 min. | Cooking Time: 60-70 min. | Servings: 2

Ingredients:

15 oz goat ribs

10 sweet potatoes, peeled and spiralized

1 squash, peeled and spiralized

10 garlic cloves, minced

7 tablespoons Olive oil

salt and pepper

2 teaspoons basil

1 teaspoon powdered black pepper

1 teaspoon powdered red pepper

2 tablespoons powdered garlic

5 tablespoons freshly squeezed lemon juice

1 bunch of fresh chives, chopped

How to Prepare:

1. Combine the powdered black pepper, red pepper, powdered garlic, basil, some salt and pepper. Season the goat ribs with the salt and pepper, and toss in the powdered garlic, basil, and pepper mix. Then sprinkle the lemon juice on top. Marinate the goat ribs 24 hours in the powdered garlic, pepper, basil, and lemon juice.

2. Heat the Olive oil and fry, then stew the goat ribs for 60-70 minutes. 20 minutes before the meat is ready, mix in the spiralized squash and stew with the ribs with the lid closed for around 10 minutes, until the liquid is absorbed. A few minutes before the goat ribs are ready, mix in the minced garlic cloves.

3. Meanwhile, in a second skillet or wok, fry the spiralized sweet potatoes. Fry the sweet potatoes for around 20 minutes, until golden brown.

4. Sprinkle the chopped chives and you are free to serve the juicy goat ribs with the spiralized sweet

potatoes, squash and fresh greenery. Remember that this dish could be served warm.

Nutritional Information:

Calories: 364; Total fat: 64 oz; Total carbohydrates: 79 oz; Protein: 39 oz

Inspiralized Zucchini with Goat, Onions and Porter Beer

Prep Time: 20 min. | Cooking Time: 60-70 min. | Servings: 3

Ingredients:

25 oz goat meat, cubed

3 bottles of dark beer, Porter or Belgian Style Beer with coriander (Chinese parsley)

7 big onions, peeled and chopped

5 tablespoons, white flour

1 cup of tomato sauce

2 cups of peanuts

2 big zucchinis, peeled and spiralized

7 tablespoons Olive oil

7 tablespoons freshly squeezed lemon juice

1 teaspoon powdered red pepper

2 tablespoons powdered garlic

1 teaspoon nutmeg & basil, ground

salt and pepper

How to Prepare:

1. Preheat the oven to 225°-245° Fahrenheit and roast the peanuts in the oven for around 10-15 minutes until lightly browned and crispy, then grind the peanuts using a food processor.

2. In a bowl, combine the powdered red pepper, powdered garlic, nutmeg, basil, some salt and pepper, mix well. Season the goat meat cubes with the salt and pepper, and toss in the powdered garlic, powdered red pepper, basil, onions and nutmeg mix. Set the meat aside to marinate it overnight in Porter or Belgian Style Beer with the coriander, onions and spices.

3. Preheat the oven to 330°-350° Fahrenheit, and bake the cubed goat meat for around 60-70 minutes until golden brown and crispy. Toss the spiralized zucchini in the Olive oil, tomato sauce, white flour and salt. 10-15 minutes before the goat meat is

ready mix in the spiralized zucchini and bake it with the goat chunks.

4. Spoon the peanuts over the spiralized zucchini and baked goat chunks, sprinkle the salt and pepper and pour the freshly squeezed lemon juice over the meat. You are free to serve the spiralized zucchini with the goat in separate plates with a cold beer. Remember that this dish should be served warm.

Nutritional Information:

Calories: 362; Total fat: 52 oz; Total carbohydrates: 72 oz; Protein: 39 oz

Goat Ribs in Garlic Mayonnaise with Walnuts and Spiralized Zucchini

Prep Time: 25 min. | Cooking Time: 60-70 min. | Servings: 2

Ingredients:

15 oz goat ribs

2 cups of walnuts

3 cups of garlic mayonnaise

1 zucchini, peeled and spiralized

5 tomatoes, cubed

6 garlic cloves, minced

5 tablespoons Olive oil

5 tablespoons soy sauce

7 tablespoons freshly squeezed lemon juice

1 teaspoon powdered chili pepper

3 tablespoons powdered garlic

salt and pepper

How to Prepare:

1. Preheat the oven to 225°-245° Fahrenheit and roast the walnuts in the oven for around 10 minutes until lightly browned and crispy.

2. In a bowl, combine powdered chili pepper, powdered garlic, pepper and some salt. Season the goat meat with the salt and pepper, and toss in the powdered garlic and powdered chili pepper mix. Spoon the garlic mayonnaise over the goat meat and marinate the meat 24 hours in spices and mayonnaise.

3. Heat the Olive oil in a frying pan or wok and stew the goat ribs for around 20 minutes. Preheat the oven to 335°-345° Fahrenheit, and bake the ribs for around 40-50 minutes until golden brown. Toss the spiralized zucchini in the Olive oil and salt. 10 minutes before the goat is ready add in the spiralized zucchini and bake it with the goat ribs.

4. Combine the soy sauce with the cubed tomatoes, walnuts and minced garlic cloves and spoon over the spiralized zucchini and goat ribs.

5. Sprinkle the salt and pepper and pour the freshly squeezed lemon juice over the spiralized zucchini and goat ribs and you are free to serve the spiralized zucchini and goat meat in separate plates. Remember that this dish should be served warm.

Nutritional Information:

Calories: 364; Total fat: 64 oz; Total carbohydrates: 77 oz; Protein: 49 oz

Goat Meat in Wine, with Onions and Inspiralized Zucchini

Prep Time: 20 min. | Cooking Time: 60-70 min. | Servings: 3

Ingredients:

25 oz goat meat, cubed

1 bottle of white wine

7 big onions, peeled and chopped

5 tablespoons, white flour

1 cup of tomato sauce

2 cups of peanuts

2 big zucchinis, peeled and spiralized

7 tablespoons Olive oil

7 tablespoons freshly squeezed lemon juice

1 teaspoon powdered red pepper

2 tablespoons powdered garlic

1 teaspoon nutmeg & basil, ground

salt and pepper

How to Prepare:

1. Preheat the oven to 225°-245° Fahrenheit and roast the peanuts in the oven for around 10-15 minutes until lightly browned and crispy, then grind the peanuts using a food processor.

2. In a bowl, combine the powdered red pepper, powdered garlic, nutmeg, basil, some salt and pepper, mix well. Season the goat meat cubes with the salt and pepper, and toss in the powdered garlic, powdered red pepper, basil, onions and nutmeg mix. Set the meat aside to marinate it overnight in the white wine, onions and spices.

3. Preheat the oven to 330°-350° Fahrenheit, and bake the cubed goat meat for around 60-70 minutes until golden brown and crispy. Toss the spiralized zucchini in the Olive oil and salt. 10-15 minutes before the goat meat is ready mix in the spiralized zucchini, tomato sauce and white flour and bake it with the goat chunks.

4. Spoon the peanuts over the spiralized zucchini and baked goat chunks, sprinkle the salt and pepper and pour the freshly squeezed lemon juice over the meat. You are free to serve the spiralized zucchini with the goat meat in separate plates. Remember that this dish should be served warm.

Nutritional Information:

Calories: 371; Total fat: 60 oz; Total carbohydrates: 70 oz; Protein: 40 oz

Grilled Goat Ribs in Garlic Mayonnaise with Spiralized Zucchini and Celery

---

Prep Time: 35 min. | Cooking Time: 50-60 min. | Servings: 3

Ingredients:

20 oz goat ribs

2 cups of garlic mayonnaise

1 zucchini, peeled and spiralized

3 cups of celery, spiralized

5 tablespoons Olive oil

3 tablespoons soy sauce

5 tablespoons freshly squeezed lemon juice

1 teaspoon powdered chili pepper

2 tablespoons powdered garlic

nutmeg

salt and pepper

How to Prepare:

1. In a bowl, combine powdered chili pepper, powdered garlic, nutmeg, some salt and pepper. Season the goat ribs with the salt and pepper, and toss in the powdered garlic, garlic mayonnaise and powdered chili pepper mix. Place the goat ribs into a pot or bowl and marinate the meat overnight in garlic mayonnaise and spices.

2. Toss the spiralized zucchini and celery in the Olive oil and salt. Heat the Olive oil in a frying pan or wok and fry the spiralized zucchini and celery for around 10 minutes until soft and then stew with the lid closed for around 10 minutes until the liquid is absorbed.

3. Grill the goat ribs until golden brown and crispy. Spoon the soy sauce over the grilled goat ribs. Then spoon the spiralized zucchini and celery on top.

4. Sprinkle the salt and pepper and pour the freshly squeezed lemon juice over the spiralized zucchini and grilled goat ribs and you are free to serve the

grilled meat. Remember that this dish should be served warm.

Nutritional Information:

Calories: 359; Total fat: 79 oz; Total carbohydrates: 89 oz; Protein: 57 oz

Grilled Lamb Ribs in Garlic Mayonnaise with Garlic and Spiralized Zucchini

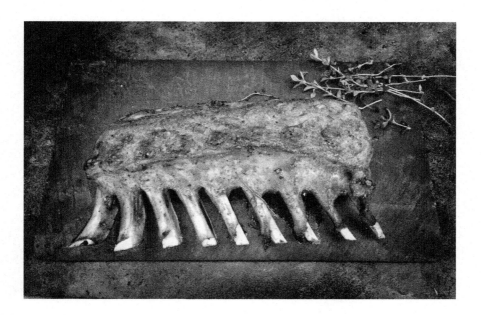

Prep Time: 35 min. | Cooking Time: 60-70 min. | Servings: 3

Ingredients:

20 oz lamb ribs

2 cups of garlic mayonnaise

1 zucchini, peeled and spiralized

10 garlic cloves, minced

5 tablespoons Olive oil

3 tablespoons soy sauce

5 tablespoons freshly squeezed lemon juice

1 teaspoon powdered chili pepper

2 tablespoons powdered garlic

nutmeg

salt and pepper

How to Prepare:

1. In a bowl, combine powdered chili pepper, powdered garlic, nutmeg, garlic, some salt and pepper. Season the lamb ribs with the salt and pepper, and toss in the garlic, powdered garlic, garlic mayonnaise and powdered chili pepper mix. Place the lamb ribs into a pot or bowl and marinate the meat overnight in garlic mayonnaise and spices.

2. Toss the spiralized zucchini in the Olive oil and salt. Heat the Olive oil in a frying pan or wok and fry the spiralized zucchini for around 10 minutes until soft and then stew with the lid closed for around 10 minutes until the liquid is absorbed.

3. Grill the lamb ribs until golden brown and crispy. Spoon the soy sauce over the grilled lamb ribs. Then spoon the spiralized zucchini on top.

4. Sprinkle the salt and pepper and pour the freshly squeezed lemon juice over the spiralized zucchini and grilled lamb ribs and you are free to serve the grilled meat. Remember that this dish should be served warm.

Nutritional Information:

Calories: 381; Total fat: 82 oz; Total carbohydrates: 95 oz; Protein: 60 oz

Lamb Meat in Wine, with Onions and Spiralized Zucchini

Prep Time: 20 min. | Cooking Time: 60-70 min. | Servings: 3

Ingredients:

20 oz lamb meat, cubed

1 bottle of white wine

8 onions, peeled and chopped

5 tablespoons, white flour

2 cups of peanuts

2 big zucchinis, peeled and spiralized

7 tablespoons Olive oil

7 tablespoons freshly squeezed lemon juice

1 teaspoon powdered red pepper

2 tablespoons powdered garlic

1 teaspoon nutmeg & basil, ground

salt and pepper

How to Prepare:

1. Preheat the oven to 225°-245° Fahrenheit and roast the peanuts in the oven for around 10-15 minutes until lightly browned and crispy, then grind the peanuts using a food processor.

2. In a bowl, combine the powdered red pepper, powdered garlic, nutmeg, basil, some salt and pepper, mix well. Season the lamb meat cubes with the salt and pepper, and toss in the powdered garlic, powdered red pepper, basil, onions and nutmeg mix. Set the meat aside to marinate it overnight in the white wine, onions and spices.

3. Preheat the oven to 330°-350° Fahrenheit, and bake the cubed lamb meat for around 60-70 minutes until golden brown and crispy. Toss the spiralized zucchini in the Olive oil and salt. 10-15 minutes before the lamb meat is ready mix in the spiralized zucchini and white flour and bake it with the lamb chunks.

4. Spoon the peanuts over the spiralized zucchini and baked lamb chunks, sprinkle the salt and pepper and pour the freshly squeezed lemon juice over the meat. You are free to serve the spiralized zucchini with the lamb meat in separate plates. Remember that this dish should be served warm.

Nutritional Information:

Calories: 375; Total fat: 69 oz; Total carbohydrates: 75 oz; Protein: 42 oz

Spiralized Cabbage with Lamb, Garlic and Beer

Prep Time: 20 min. | Cooking Time: 60-70 min. | Servings: 3

Ingredients:

25 oz lamb meat, cubed

1 cabbage, spiralized

3 bottles of dark Porter Beer or use Belgian Style Beer with coriander (Chinese parsley)

10 garlic cloves, minced

5 tablespoons, white flour

1 cup of tomato sauce

2 cups of peanuts

7 tablespoons Olive oil

7 tablespoons freshly squeezed lemon juice

1 teaspoon powdered red pepper

2 tablespoons powdered garlic

1 teaspoon nutmeg & basil, ground

salt and pepper

How to Prepare:

1. Preheat the oven to 225°-245° Fahrenheit and roast the peanuts in the oven for around 10-15 minutes until lightly browned and crispy, then grind the peanuts using a food processor.

2. In a bowl, combine the minced garlic, powdered red pepper, powdered garlic, nutmeg, basil, some salt and pepper, mix well. Season the lamb meat cubes with the salt and pepper, and toss in the powdered garlic, powdered red pepper, basil, onions and nutmeg mix. Set the meat aside to marinate it overnight in Porter or Belgian Style Beer with the coriander, garlic and spices.

3. Preheat the oven to 330°-350° Fahrenheit, and bake the cubed lamb meat for around 60-70 minutes until golden brown and crispy. Toss the spiralized cabbage in the Olive oil, tomato sauce, white flour and salt. 10-15 minutes before the lamb meat is ready mix in the spiralized cabbage and bake it with the lamb chunks.

4. Spoon the peanuts over the spiralized zucchini and baked lamb chunks, sprinkle the salt and pepper and pour the freshly squeezed lemon juice over the meat. You are free to serve the spiralized zucchini with the lamb in separate plates with a cold beer. Remember that this dish should be served warm.

Nutritional Information:

Calories: 369; Total fat: 68 oz; Total carbohydrates: 81 oz; Protein: 41 oz

Grilled Pork Belly with Garlic, Spiralized Squash and Pineapple

Prep Time: 30 min. | Cooking Time: 60-70 min. | Servings: 4

Ingredients:

20 oz pork belly, cubed

1 squash, peeled and spiralized

1 pineapple, peeled and spiralized

10 garlic cloves, minced

5 tablespoons Olive oil

4 tablespoons soy sauce

5 tablespoons freshly squeezed lemon juice

1 teaspoon powdered chili pepper

2 tablespoons powdered garlic

nutmeg

salt and pepper

How to Prepare:

1. In a bowl, combine powdered chili pepper, powdered garlic, nutmeg, garlic, some salt and pepper. Season the pork belly with the salt and pepper, and toss in the garlic, powdered garlic, nutmeg, and powdered chili pepper mix. Place the pork into a pot and marinate the meat overnight in spices.

2. Toss the spiralized squash in the Olive oil and salt. Heat the Olive oil in a frying pan or wok and fry the spiralized squash with the pineapple for around 10 minutes until soft and then stew with the lid closed for around 10 minutes until the liquid is absorbed.

3. Grill the pork until golden brown and crispy. Pour the soy sauce over the grilled pork. Then spoon the spiralized squash and pineapple on top.

4. Sprinkle the salt and pepper and pour the freshly squeezed lemon juice over the spiralized squash, pineapple and grilled pork and you are free to serve the grilled meat. Remember that this dish should be served warm with the cold beer.

Nutritional Information:

Calories: 384; Total fat: 83 oz; Total carbohydrates: 96 oz; Protein: 64 oz

Grilled Pork Belly with Garlic, Spiralized Squash and Oranges

---

Prep Time: 30 min. | Cooking Time: 60-70 min. | Servings: 4

Ingredients:

20 oz pork belly, cubed

1 squash, peeled and spiralized

5 oranges, peeled and cubed

10 garlic cloves, minced

5 tablespoons Olive oil

4 tablespoons soy sauce

5 tablespoons freshly squeezed lemon juice

1 teaspoon powdered chili pepper

2 tablespoons powdered garlic

nutmeg

salt and pepper

How to Prepare:

1. In a bowl, combine powdered chili pepper, powdered garlic, nutmeg, garlic, some salt and pepper. Season the pork belly with the salt and pepper, and toss in the garlic, powdered garlic, nutmeg, and powdered chili pepper mix. Place the pork into a pot and marinate the meat overnight in spices.

2. Toss the spiralized squash in the Olive oil and salt. Heat the Olive oil in a frying pan or wok and fry the spiralized squash with the cubed oranges for around 10 minutes until soft and then stew with the lid closed for around 10 minutes until the liquid is absorbed.

3. Grill the pork until golden brown and crispy. Pour the soy sauce over the grilled pork. Then spoon the spiralized squash and oranges on top.

4. Sprinkle the salt and pepper and pour the freshly squeezed lemon juice over the spiralized squash, oranges and grilled pork and you are free to serve

the grilled meat. Remember that this dish should be served warm with the cold beer.

Nutritional Information:

Calories: 380; Total fat: 80 oz; Total carbohydrates: 92 oz; Protein: 60 oz

Grilled Pork Belly with Garlic, Spiralized Zucchini and Cashews

---

Prep Time: 30 min. | Cooking Time: 60-70 min. | Servings: 4

Ingredients:

20 oz pork belly, cubed

1 zucchini, peeled and spiralized

1 cup of cashews

10 garlic cloves, minced

5 tablespoons Olive oil

4 tablespoons soy sauce

5 tablespoons freshly squeezed lemon juice

1 teaspoon powdered chili pepper

2 tablespoons powdered garlic

nutmeg

salt and pepper

How to Prepare:

1. Preheat the oven to 230°-240° Fahrenheit and roast the cashews in the oven for around 10-15 minutes until lightly browned and crispy, then grind the cashews using a food processor.

2. In a bowl, combine powdered chili pepper, powdered garlic, nutmeg, garlic, some salt and pepper. Season the pork belly with the salt and pepper, and toss in the garlic, powdered garlic, nutmeg, and powdered chili pepper mix. Place the pork into a pot and marinate the meat overnight in spices.

3. Toss the spiralized zucchini in the Olive oil and salt. Heat the Olive oil in a frying pan or wok and fry the spiralized zucchini for around 10 minutes until soft and then stew with the lid closed for around 10 minutes until the liquid is absorbed.

4. Grill the pork until golden brown and crispy. Pour the soy sauce over the grilled pork. Then spoon the spiralized zucchini and cashews on top.

5. Sprinkle the salt and pepper and pour the freshly squeezed lemon juice over the cashews, spiralized zucchini and grilled pork and you are free to serve the grilled meat. Remember that this dish should be served warm with the cold beer.

Nutritional Information:

Calories: 384; Total fat: 83 oz; Total carbohydrates: 96 oz; Protein: 64 oz

Grilled Flank Steak with Garlic, Spiralized Zucchini and Peanuts

Prep Time: 30 min. | Cooking Time: 60-70 min. | Servings: 4

Ingredients:

20 oz flank steak

1 zucchini, peeled and spiralized

15 garlic cloves, minced

1 cup of peanuts

5 tablespoons Olive oil

4 tablespoons soy sauce

5 tablespoons freshly squeezed lemon juice

1 teaspoon powdered chili pepper

2 tablespoons powdered garlic

nutmeg

salt and pepper

How to Prepare:

1. Preheat the oven to 245°-255° Fahrenheit and roast the peanuts in the oven for around 10-15 minutes until lightly browned and crispy.

2. In a bowl, combine powdered chili pepper, powdered garlic, nutmeg, garlic, some salt and pepper. Season the flank steak with the salt and pepper, and toss in the garlic, powdered garlic, nutmeg, and powdered chili pepper mix. Place the flank steak into a pot and marinate the meat overnight in spices.

3. Toss the spiralized zucchini in the Olive oil and salt. Heat the Olive oil in a frying pan or wok and fry the

spiralized zucchini for around 10 minutes and then stew with the lid closed for around 10 minutes until the liquid is absorbed.

4. Grill the meat until golden brown and crispy. Pour the soy sauce over the grilled flank steak. Then spoon the spiralized zucchini and peanuts on top.

5. Sprinkle the salt and pepper and pour the freshly squeezed lemon juice over the peanuts, spiralized zucchini and grilled flank steak and you are free to serve the grilled meat. Remember that this dish should be served warm with the cold beer.

Nutritional Information:

Calories: 386; Total fat: 84 oz; Total carbohydrates: 97 oz; Protein: 65 oz

Grilled Flank Steak In Wine with Spiralized Zucchini and Walnuts

---

Prep Time: 30 min. | Cooking Time: 60-70 min. | Servings: 4

Ingredients:

20 oz flank steak

1 bottle of white wine

1 zucchini, peeled and spiralized

8 garlic cloves, minced

1 cup of walnuts

6 tablespoons Olive oil

5 tablespoons soy sauce

7 tablespoons freshly squeezed lemon juice

2 teaspoons powdered chili pepper

2 tablespoons powdered garlic

basil

salt and pepper

How to Prepare:

1. Preheat the oven to 245°-255° Fahrenheit and roast the walnuts in the oven for around 10-15 minutes until lightly browned and crispy.

2. In a bowl, combine powdered chili pepper, powdered garlic, basil, garlic, some salt and pepper. Season the flank steak with the salt and pepper, and toss in the garlic, powdered garlic, basil, and powdered chili pepper mix. Place the flank steak into a pot and marinate the meat overnight in wine and spices.

3. Toss the spiralized zucchini in the Olive oil and salt. Heat the Olive oil in a frying pan or wok and fry the spiralized zucchini for around 10 minutes and then stew with the lid closed for around 10 minutes until the liquid is absorbed.

4. Grill the meat until golden brown and crispy. Pour the soy sauce over the grilled flank steak. Then spoon the spiralized zucchini and walnuts on top.

5. Sprinkle the salt and pepper and pour the freshly squeezed lemon juice over the walnuts, spiralized zucchini and grilled flank steak and you are free to serve the grilled meat. Remember that this dish should be served warm with the cold beer.

Nutritional Information:

Calories: 385; Total fat: 82 oz; Total carbohydrates: 94 oz; Protein: 62 oz

Spiralized Zucchini with Flank Steak, Squash and Peanuts

Prep Time: 25 min. | Cooking Time: 50-60 min. | Servings: 4

Ingredients:

25 oz flank steak

2 zucchinis, peeled and spiralized

1 squash, peeled and spiralized

2 cups of peanuts

5 garlic cloves, minced

5 tablespoons Olive oil

salt and pepper

2 teaspoons powdered black pepper

2 teaspoons powdered red pepper

4 tablespoons powdered garlic

5 tablespoons freshly squeezed lemon juice

1 bunch of fresh chives, chopped

How to Prepare:

1. Preheat the oven to 230°-260° Fahrenheit and roast the peanuts in the oven for around 10 minutes until lightly browned and crispy.

2. Combine the powdered black pepper, red pepper, powdered garlic and some salt. Season the flank steak with the salt and pepper, and toss in the powdered garlic, and pepper mix. Then pour the lemon juice on top. Marinate the meat overnight in the powdered garlic, pepper, and lemon juice.

3. Heat the oil and fry the meat for 50-60 minutes. 10 minutes before the meat is ready, mix in the spiralized squash and stew with the flank steak with the lid closed for around 10 minutes, until the liquid is absorbed. A few minutes before the meat is ready, mix in the minced garlic cloves.

4. Meanwhile, in a second skillet or wok, stew the spiralized zucchini. Stew the zucchini for around 10-20 minutes.

5. Mix in the peanuts. Sprinkle the chopped chives and you are free to serve the flank steak with the spiralized zucchini and the fresh greenery. Remember that this dish could be served warm.

Nutritional Information:

Calories: 370; Total fat: 89 oz; Total carbohydrates: 108 oz; Protein: 77 oz

Grilled Rib Eye Steak In Beer with Spiralized Squash and Pineapple

Prep Time: 25 min. | Cooking Time: 50-60 min. | Servings: 4

Ingredients:

20 oz rib eye steak

3 bottles of beer

1 squash, peeled and spiralized

1 pineapple, peeled and spiralized

8 garlic cloves, minced

1 cup of walnuts

6 tablespoons Olive oil

5 tablespoons soy sauce

7 tablespoons freshly squeezed lemon juice

2 teaspoons powdered chili pepper

2 tablespoons powdered garlic

basil

salt and pepper

How to Prepare:

1. Preheat the oven to 245°-255° Fahrenheit and roast the walnuts in the oven for around 10-15 minutes until lightly browned and crispy.

2. In a bowl, combine powdered chili pepper, powdered garlic, basil, garlic, some salt and pepper. Season the rib eye steak with the salt and pepper, and toss in the garlic, powdered garlic, basil, and powdered chili pepper mix. Place the rib eye steak into a pot and marinate the meat overnight in beer and spices.

3. Toss the spiralized squash in the Olive oil and salt. Heat the Olive oil in a frying pan or wok and fry the spiralized squash with the pineapple for around 10 minutes and then stew with the lid closed for around 10 minutes until the liquid is absorbed.

4. Grill the meat until golden brown and crispy. Pour the soy sauce over the grilled rib eye steak. Then spoon the spiralized squash, pineapple and walnuts on top.

5. Sprinkle the salt and pepper and pour the freshly squeezed lemon juice over the spiralized squash, pineapple and grilled rib eye steak and you are free to serve the grilled meat. Remember that this dish should be served warm with the fresh salad.

Nutritional Information:

Calories: 388; Total fat: 89 oz; Total carbohydrates: 97 oz; Protein: 69 oz

Grilled Sirloin Steak with Garlic, Spiralized Squash and Oranges

---

Prep Time: 30 min. | Cooking Time: 60-70 min. | Servings: 4

Ingredients:

20 sirloin steak

1 squash, peeled and spiralized

5 oranges, peeled and cubed

12 garlic cloves, minced

5 tablespoons Olive oil

4 tablespoons soy sauce

5 tablespoons freshly squeezed lemon juice

1 teaspoon powdered chili pepper

2 tablespoons powdered garlic

nutmeg

salt and pepper

How to Prepare:

1. In a bowl, combine powdered chili pepper, powdered garlic, nutmeg, garlic, some salt and pepper. Season the sirloin steak with the salt and pepper, and toss in the garlic, powdered garlic, nutmeg, and powdered chili pepper mix. Place the sirloin steak into a pot and marinate the meat overnight in spices.

2. Toss the spiralized squash in the Olive oil and salt. Heat the Olive oil in a frying pan or wok and fry the spiralized squash with the cubed oranges for around 10 minutes until soft and then stew with the lid closed for around 10 minutes until the liquid is absorbed.

3. Grill the sirloin steak until golden brown and crispy. Pour the soy sauce over the grilled meat. Then spoon the spiralized squash and oranges on top.

4. Sprinkle the salt and pepper and pour the freshly squeezed lemon juice over the spiralized squash, oranges and grilled sirloin steak and you are free to

serve the grilled meat. Remember that this dish should be served warm with the cold beer.

Nutritional Information:

Calories: 387; Total fat: 89 oz; Total carbohydrates: 115 oz; Protein: 75 oz

Spiralized Cabbage with Lamb Ribs, Garlic and Beer

Prep Time: 35 min. | Cooking Time: 60-70 min. | Servings: 4

Ingredients:

25 oz lamb ribs

1 cabbage, spiralized

4 bottles of dark Porter Beer or use Belgian Style Beer with coriander (Chinese parsley)

10 garlic cloves, minced

5 tablespoons, white flour

1 cup of tomato sauce

2 cups of peanuts

7 tablespoons Olive oil

7 tablespoons freshly squeezed lemon juice

1 teaspoon powdered red pepper

2 tablespoons powdered garlic

1 teaspoon nutmeg & basil, ground

salt and pepper

How to Prepare:

1. Preheat the oven to 225°-245° Fahrenheit and roast the peanuts in the oven for around 10-15 minutes until lightly browned and crispy, then grind the peanuts using a food processor.

2. In a bowl, combine the minced garlic, powdered red pepper, powdered garlic, nutmeg, basil, some salt and pepper, mix well. Season the lamb meat with the salt and pepper, and toss in the powdered garlic, powdered red pepper, basil, garlic and nutmeg mix. Set the meat aside to marinate it overnight in Porter or Belgian Style Beer with the coriander, garlic and spices.

3. Preheat the oven to 330°-350° Fahrenheit, and bake the lamb ribs for around 60-70 minutes until golden brown and crispy. Toss the spiralized cabbage in the Olive oil, tomato sauce, white flour and salt. 10-15 minutes before the lamb meat is

ready mix in the spiralized cabbage and bake it with the lamb ribs.

4. Spoon the peanuts over the spiralized cabbage and baked lamb ribs, sprinkle the salt and pepper and pour the freshly squeezed lemon juice over the meat. You are free to serve the spiralized cabbage with the lamb in separate plates with a cold beer. Remember that this dish should be served warm.

Nutritional Information:

Calories: 379; Total fat: 78 oz; Total carbohydrates: 87 oz; Protein: 65 oz

Cucumber Zoodles with Pork Meatballs, Hazelnuts and Beer (Cover Recipe)

Prep Time: 35 min. | Cooking Time: 60-70 min. | Servings: 4

Ingredients:

20 pork meatballs

2 cups of hazelnuts

5 cucumbers, peeled and spiralized

4 bottles of dark Porter Beer or use Belgian Style Beer

1 squash, spiralized

7 garlic cloves, minced

5 tablespoons, white flour

7 tablespoons Olive oil

7 tablespoons freshly squeezed lemon juice

1 teaspoon powdered red pepper

2 tablespoons powdered garlic

1 teaspoon nutmeg & basil, ground

salt and pepper

How to Prepare:

1. Preheat the oven to 225°-245° Fahrenheit and roast the hazelnuts in the oven for around 10-15 minutes until lightly browned and crispy, then grind the hazelnuts using a food processor.

2. In a bowl, combine the minced garlic, powdered red pepper, powdered garlic, nutmeg, basil, some salt and pepper, mix well. Season the pork meatballs with the salt and pepper, and toss in the powdered garlic, powdered red pepper, basil, garlic and

nutmeg mix. Set the meat aside to marinate it 2 hours in Porter or Belgian Style Beer with spices.

3. Preheat the oven to 330°-350° Fahrenheit, and bake the pork meatballs for around 60-70 minutes until golden brown. Toss the spiralized squash in the Olive oil, white flour and salt. 20 minutes before the pork meatballs are ready mix in the spiralized squash and bake it with the pork balls.

4. Spoon the hazelnuts and cucumbers over the spiralized squash and baked pork. Sprinkle some salt and pepper and pour the freshly squeezed lemon juice over the meatballs. You are free to serve the spiralized cucumbers and squash with the pork meatballs and Olives. Remember that this dish should be served warm.

Nutritional Information:

Calories: 379; Total fat: 78 oz; Total carbohydrates: 87 oz; Protein: 65 oz

Grilled Mahi-Mahi Fish with Garlic, Spiralized Squash and Oranges

---

Prep Time: 30 min. | Cooking Time: 40-50 min. | Servings: 4

Ingredients:

20 oz mahi-mahi fish, cubed

1 squash, peeled and spiralized

5 oranges, peeled and cubed

10 garlic cloves, minced

5 tablespoons Olive oil

4 tablespoons soy sauce

5 tablespoons freshly squeezed lemon juice

1 teaspoon powdered chili pepper

2 tablespoons powdered garlic

nutmeg

salt and pepper

How to Prepare:

1. In a bowl, combine powdered chili pepper, powdered garlic, nutmeg, garlic, some salt and pepper. Season the mahi-mahi fish with the salt and pepper, and toss in the garlic, powdered garlic, nutmeg, and powdered chili pepper mix. Place the fish into a pot and marinate the mahi-mahi cubes overnight in spices.

2. Toss the spiralized squash in the Olive oil and salt. Heat the Olive oil in a frying pan or wok and fry the spiralized squash with the cubed oranges for around 10 minutes until soft and then stew with the lid closed for around 10 minutes until the liquid is absorbed.

3. Grill the fish until golden brown and crispy. Pour the soy sauce over the grilled mahi-mahi fish. Then spoon the spiralized squash and oranges on top.

4. Sprinkle the salt and pepper and pour the freshly squeezed lemon juice over the spiralized squash, oranges and grilled mahi-mahi. Now you are free to

serve the grilled fish. Remember that this dish should be served warm with the beer or wine.

Nutritional Information:

Calories: 299; Total fat: 68 oz; Total carbohydrates: 79 oz; Protein: 49 oz

Conclusion

Thank you for buying this spiralizer cookbook. I hope this was able to help you prepare tasty spiralizer recipes. This fifth spiralizer recipe book includes various spiralizer recipes with fish and meat. You can prepare these recipes for yourself or your family. **Thank you** and I hope you have enjoyed this.

If you've enjoyed this cookbook, I'd greatly appreciate if you could leave an honest opinion.

Your opinions are very important to us authors, and it only takes a minute for you to post or contact me directly.

Your direct feedback could be used to help other readers to discover the advantages of spiralizer recipes!

If you have anything you want me to know, any questions, suggestions or feedback, please don't hesitate to contact me directly, through my Facebook page.

Thank you again and I hope you have enjoyed spiralizer cookbook.

Recipe Index

Printed in Great Britain
by Amazon

27416687R00064